* Animal Rescue *

BAT HOSPITAL

Clare Hibbert

W
FRANKLIN WATTS
LONDON • SYDNEY

First published in 2015 by Franklin Watts

Franklin Watts
338 Euston Road
London
NW1 3BH

Franklin Watts Australia
Level 17/207 Kent Street, Sydney, NSW 2000

Produced by Arcturus Publishing Limited,
26/27 Bickels Yard, 151–153 Bermondsey
Street, London SE1 3HA

Editor: Joe Harris
Picture researcher: Clare Hibbert
Designer: Tokiko Morishima

Picture credits:
All interior images supplied by Jurgen Freund/
Nature Picture Library, except background
images on pages 12, 14–15, 20, 23, 26–27:
Shutterstock. Cover image: Nature PL
(Jurgen Freund).

A CIP catalogue record for this book is
available from the British Library.

Dewey Decimal Classification Number:
639.9'794

ISBN: 978 1 4451 3389 8

Franklin Watts is a division of Hachette
Children's Books, an Hachette UK company.
www.hachette.co.uk

Printed in China

SL003931UK
Supplier 03, Date 1014, Print Run 3572

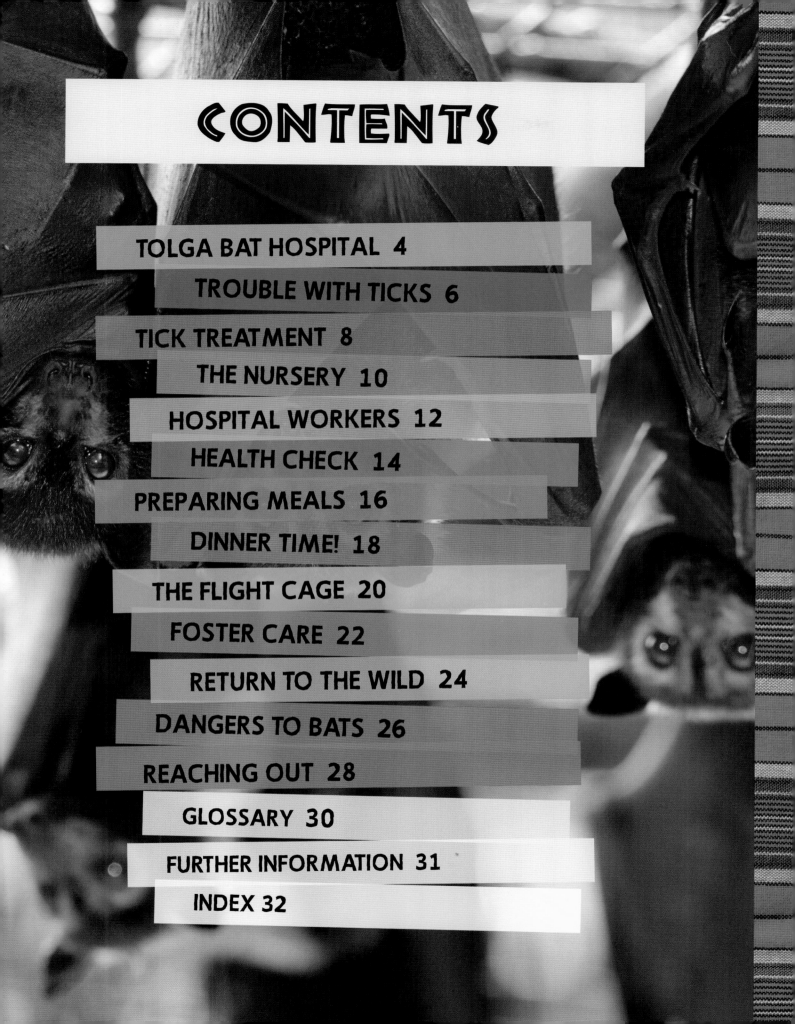

CONTENTS

TOLGA BAT HOSPITAL

In a remote part of Queensland, Australia, is a very special hospital — Tolga Bat Hospital. It is named after the Tolga Scrub, the area of rainforest where it is found. Its patients are sick, injured or orphaned flying foxes.

The Tolga Scrub is an important habitat for flying foxes, also known as fruit bats. These amazing animals are the largest kind of bat in the world. They have big eyes and doglike faces. Spectacled flying foxes roost in the canopy (the highest branches) in the Tolga Scrub. There are also black flying foxes and little red flying foxes.

Bats roost in the flight cage at Tolga Bat Hospital.

Tolga

AUSTRALIA · Tolga Bat Hospital

Jenny Maclean set up the Tolga Bat Hospital in 1997. She bought a two-hectare (five-acre) area of the forest and began to grow native plants on the land to help conserve it. She still runs the hospital and is passionate about saving bats and protecting Australian wildlife. At first, her hospital worked only with flying foxes. Today it looks after many different kinds of bat.

TROUBLE WITH TICKS

In the mid-1980s, large numbers of spectacled flying foxes began dying mysteriously. Dozens of dead and dying animals were found on the forest floor. Scientists warned that spectacled flying foxes were a threatened species, at risk of extinction.

It was not until 1990 that two researchers, Bruce and Ann Johnson, discovered the cause of the problem. All of the dead and dying bats had been bitten by paralysis ticks. 'Paralysis' means not being able to move, and the bites were making the bats unable to open and close their feet, so they could not roost.

Fact File: Ticks

Ticks are parasites that live by sucking blood. They go through different life stages. Before each change, paralysis ticks feed on an animal's blood. Some animals, such as koalas, are immune to (not hurt by) the poisons in their bite. Flying foxes are not immune.

As more rainforest has been cut down to make way for farms, buildings and roads, there has been less food for the bats. When they leave the forest looking for food, they come into contact with the ticks. Then they carry them back to their colonies.

TICK TREATMENT

If they are found and treated in time, bats that have been bitten by paralysis ticks can recover. The hospital workers search the colony twice a day for affected bats. They take the bats back to the hospital for treatment.

The first job is to find the tick and pinch it off the bat's body. It's important not to leave any of the tick's mouthparts behind – this could cause an infection. The carers check whether the bat can be saved. If the patient is a mother bat, her pup is usually taken away to be cared for separately.

The bat's paralysis is caused by toxins from the tick's mouthparts. Hospital workers inject the sick bat with anti-toxins – drugs that can stop the poisons. They also check the animal for fly eggs or maggots. This is because flies sometimes lay their eggs on bats lying on the forest floor. Another problem is dehydration – not drinking enough. So the carers give a sick bat plenty to drink.

A hospital worker feeds sick bats fruit juice with a syringe.

THE NURSERY

Baby bats are used to being tucked safely under Mum's wings. At Tolga, the carers wrap the orphans in little blankets called swaddling cloths. It keeps them warm and stops them hurting themselves or each other with their clawed wings and feet.

Until they are eight weeks old, the orphans are fed only on milk. Just like human newborns, they must eat every two to four hours. The pups are given human baby formula or powdered cows' milk with added glucodin, a sugar that is easy to digest.

Fact File: Bat Babies

A spectacled flying fox's pregnancy lasts seven months. She gives birth to a single pup between October and December. That time of year is spring in Australia, so there should be plenty of food for Mum to eat while her body is making milk.

Older babies take their milk through rubber teats from babies' bottles. Sometimes they even sleep with a teat in their mouth! It seems to comfort them. Newborns are too tiny to feed from the rubber teats. Instead, carers drip milk into their mouths using a syringe. It takes a long time!

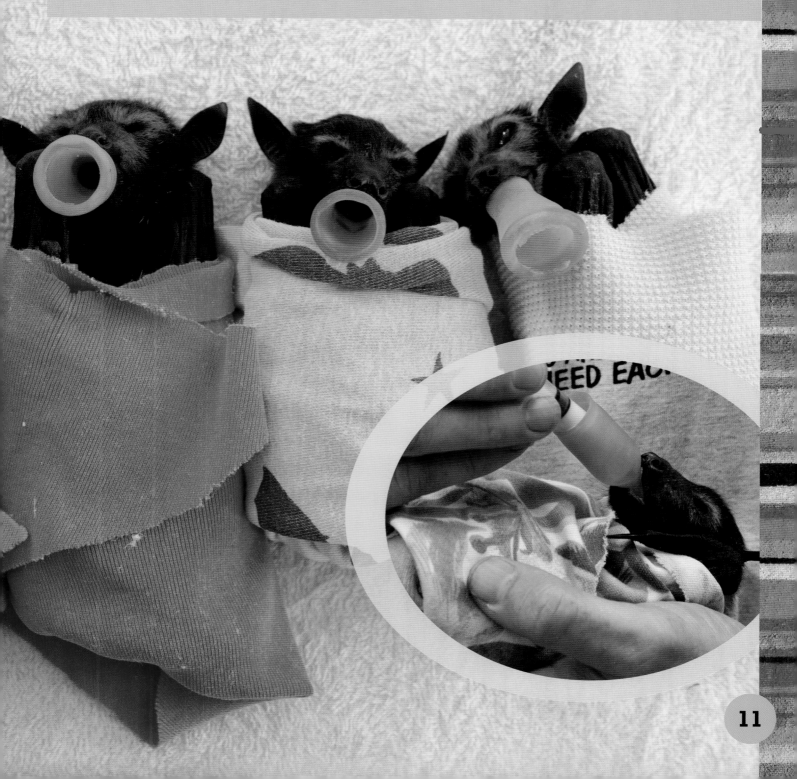

HOSPITAL WORKERS

Almost all of the staff at the hospital are volunteers. Some are students or travellers who stay at Tolga for a few weeks or months. They work for no pay but they all agree that the volunteering is very rewarding.

The hospital has one full-time member of staff and around 10 volunteers who live locally. In addition, about 35 other volunteers stay each year from around the world. Most come during the tick season, from October to February, which is also when spectacled flying foxes have their babies. This is the hospital's busiest time. The volunteers live on site in tents. It means there are people to care for the bats around the clock.

The staff work in shifts. Their jobs include handling the bats, giving them food and medicine and lots of cleaning up! They go into the forest to rescue paralysed bats and do surveys of colonies to see how wild bats are doing. They also help out by giving tours to people who visit the hospital.

HEALTH CHECK

Every bat that is brought into the hospital is given a thorough health check. Volunteers keep careful notes of their findings so they can track how each patient is doing. They quickly learn to recognise the individual bats!

The bats are weighed regularly so the hospital staff can check that they are putting on weight at the right rate. This is especially important for babies as they are still growing and developing. Swaddling makes the bats easy to weigh because they don't flap about on the scales.

The volunteers also keep notes on the bats' other measurements as they grow, such as their wingspan and their body length. Carers do everything calmly and quietly with no sudden movements. They check the animals' heartbeats for signs of stress.

A volunteer checks a bat's microchip number.

Fact File: Microchipping

The hospital microchips each bat. A tiny computer chip, the size of a grain of rice, is put under the animal's skin. Each chip has a unique number. If it's found again in the future, the bat can be identified and matched back to its medical records.

PREPARING MEALS

Flying foxes feed on fruit, flowers and sweet, honeyed nectar. In the wild, they spend all their waking hours finding food and feeding. At Tolga, the volunteers spend most of their day preparing fruit for the bats!

Most of a wild flying fox's diet is made up of tropical fruits, such as figs and guavas. Trucks arrive at Tolga laden with crates of fruit, which all need to be unloaded and stored. Volunteers chop up the fruit. Watermelons, for example, have a tough outer skin that the bats cannot bite through. Some days, more than 80 kg (175 lb) of fruit is prepared.

A volunteer carries strings of apples.

The volunteers stick chunks of fruit onto wires to hang from the bats' cages. Harder fruits, such as apples, take more effort to eat – especially if they're threaded on long wires or S-shaped hooks. 'Working' for their food stops the bats getting bored. Bananas are another favourite. Some are simply peeled and placed inside wire mesh feeders. Others are kept back for whizzing up into smoothies – delicious!

DINNER TIME!

The volunteers make sure there is food available to the bats all the time. As well as putting out fruit, they hang up leaves from mulberry and fiddlewood trees. The green leaves are full of important vitamins that the bats cannot get from fruit.

The little red flying foxes at the hospital feed mainly on nectar and pollen so the volunteers put out flowers for them. White tea tree blossom is a favourite with the bats. The hospital also has tube-nosed bats. They are fruit feeders but they can be fussy – some will only take fruit juice!

Bats are famous for echolocation – finding food in the dark using sound. Only small bats do this, however. Flying foxes rely on sight and sound to locate their food. Volunteers often hide the food in the cages. This encourages the bats to move more, speeding up their recovery.

Fact File: Bat Diets

Not all bats eat fruit. Fishing bats skim over lakes and rivers, catching fish to eat. Other species feed on frogs or on other bats and some even suck blood! Most small bat species are insectivores (they eat only insects). A pipistrelle bat can eat more than 3,000 insects a night!

THE FLIGHT CAGE

The bat orphans begin their stay at hospital in the nursery. When they get stronger, they are moved to the flight cage. There is enough space for the bats to stretch their wings and practise flying.

Some bats in the flight cage are still too injured to fly. Even so, being in the cage helps them to grow stronger by climbing and moving around. It's like an adventure playground for bats, large enough to include trees, ropes and nets! The trees give them some shade, but there are sunny areas where the flying foxes can bask, fanning themselves with their wings.

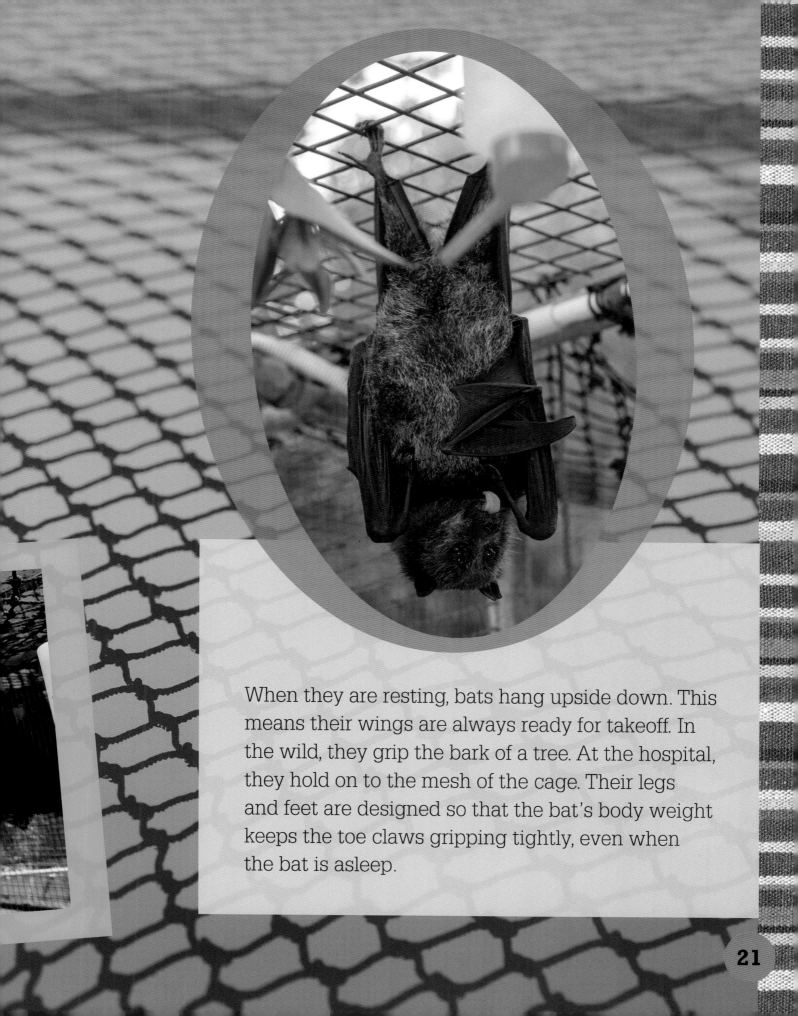

When they are resting, bats hang upside down. This means their wings are always ready for takeoff. In the wild, they grip the bark of a tree. At the hospital, they hold on to the mesh of the cage. Their legs and feet are designed so that the bat's body weight keeps the toe claws gripping tightly, even when the bat is asleep.

FOSTER CARE

In a typical season, Tolga Bat Hospital rescues about 300 orphaned bats. It doesn't have the space, staff or money to look after all of these. Around two-thirds are cared for elsewhere.

When they are bigger, stronger and nearly ready for release back into the rainforest, the fostered orphans come back to Tolga. They are transported by air in crates with mesh tops that they can grip. Each crate is divided into individual roosts, so the bats cannot claw each other.

When the bats arrive back at the hospital, the first thing the volunteers do is give them a drink. Travelling is a thirsty business! Each bat is given a health check. Once they have had time to recover from the journey, they can begin the process of returning to the wild.

Fact File: Hospital Costs
Food — for both the bats and the volunteers — is the hospital's biggest expense. There are microchips and doses of anti-toxin to buy, vets' bills to pay and general running costs. The hospital relies a lot on grants and donations. It also raises money through its visitor centre.

RETURN TO THE WILD

A few of the bats at the hospital are too injured to ever return to the wild. They will stay at the centre their whole lives. For most, though, the aim is to go back to the rainforest colony. It is a slow process.

The first stage is to move the bats to the release cage, which is in the middle of the forest near wild mothers and babies. At first, the cage is kept shut while the bats get used to the new sights, smells and sounds. After a few days, the volunteers open the cage door. This allows the bats to rejoin their wild cousins.

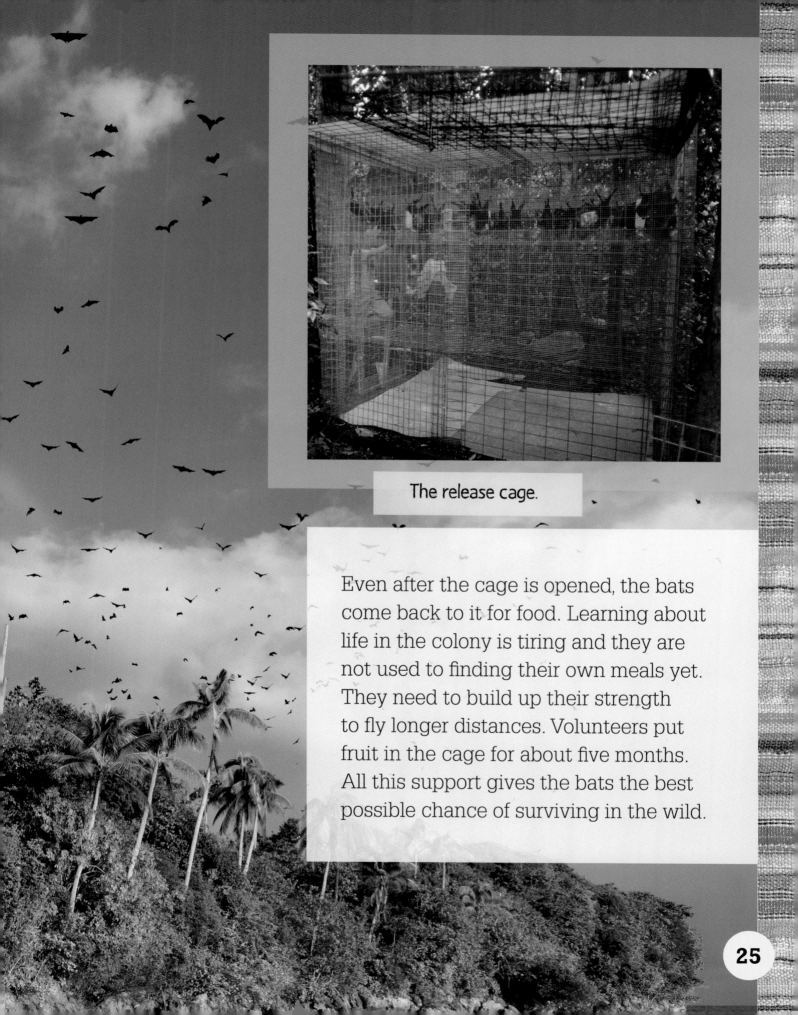

The release cage.

Even after the cage is opened, the bats come back to it for food. Learning about life in the colony is tiring and they are not used to finding their own meals yet. They need to build up their strength to fly longer distances. Volunteers put fruit in the cage for about five months. All this support gives the bats the best possible chance of surviving in the wild.

DANGERS TO BATS

At first, Jenny and the team at Tolga worked only with spectacled flying foxes that were suffering the effects of paralysis ticks. But before long they were helping other bats in need. Bats face many dangers in the wild.

Some bats go to the hospital after being caught on barbed wire or power lines. Others are found tangled up in the netting that protects farmers' crops and may have gone days without food. As long as they are found in time, the bats can be nursed back to health.

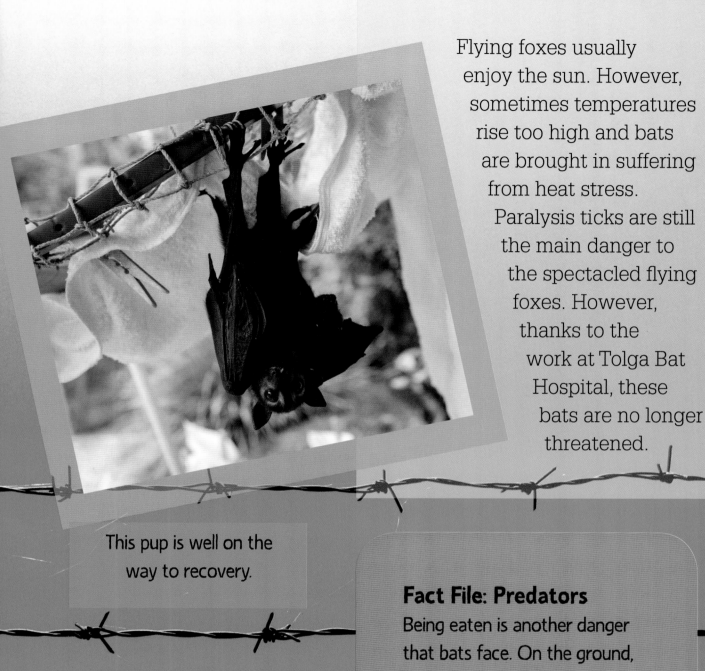

Flying foxes usually enjoy the sun. However, sometimes temperatures rise too high and bats are brought in suffering from heat stress. Paralysis ticks are still the main danger to the spectacled flying foxes. However, thanks to the work at Tolga Bat Hospital, these bats are no longer threatened.

This pup is well on the way to recovery.

Fact File: Predators

Being eaten is another danger that bats face. On the ground, flying foxes are at risk from snakes and goannas, a type of large lizard. Sea eagles or owls may take them from the trees or mid-air. Dogs and cats also kill bats if they get the chance.

REACHING OUT

As well as saving bats' lives, Tolga Bat Hospital works to teach people more about these animals. It shows people how important it is to conserve the bats' rainforest habitat. Thanks to Jenny and her team, the bats face a brighter future.

At the visitor centre, people learn about bats and the threats to them at first hand. Some people are afraid of flying foxes or think of them as pests because they strip trees of fruit and leaves. Seeing the bats up close helps people see how vulnerable they are. The centre raises much-needed funds for the hospital by charging visitors an entrance fee and selling souvenirs in its shop.

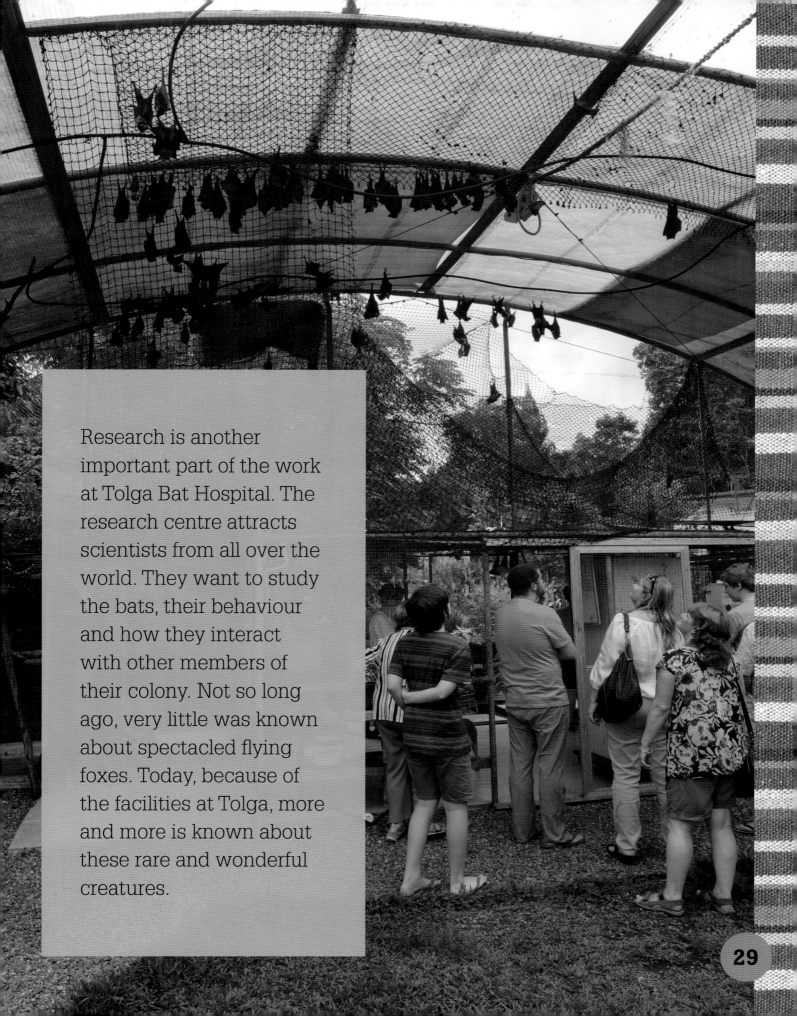

Research is another important part of the work at Tolga Bat Hospital. The research centre attracts scientists from all over the world. They want to study the bats, their behaviour and how they interact with other members of their colony. Not so long ago, very little was known about spectacled flying foxes. Today, because of the facilities at Tolga, more and more is known about these rare and wonderful creatures.

GLOSSARY

CANOPY The uppermost layer of rainforest vegetation (plant life).

COLONY A group of animals of the same species that live closely together.

CONSERVE To protect and keep for the future.

DEHYDRATION Lacking fluids.

ECHOLOCATION Detecting an object's location by producing a sound and then sensing how the echoes bounce back.

EXTINCTION Disappearing forever.

FOSTERED Brought up or cared for by someone else.

GRANT Money awarded for a special purpose, for example by a government or a charity.

HABITAT The place where an animal or plant lives.

IMMUNE Safe from a particular danger.

INFECTION A disease or condition caused by germs such as bacteria.

INTERACT Behave with one another.

NATIVE Naturally found in a place.

NECTAR A sweet liquid produced by flowers to attract animals such as bats and bees.

ORPHANED Having lost its parents. In bat society, where only mothers raise the pups, a baby that has lost its mother counts as 'orphaned'.

PARASITE An animal or plant that survives by living off another animal or plant.

PREDATOR An animal that survives by hunting, killing and eating other animals.

RAINFOREST A thick tropical forest where there is heavy rainfall.

SHIFT The time that a person works.

SWADDLING Wrapping in a blanket.

THREATENED Describes a species of animal on its way to becoming endangered (at risk of dying out completely) in the future.

TICK A bloodsucking parasite belonging to the arachnid family, related to spiders.

VOLUNTEER Someone who works for free. Volunteers at Tonga are not paid but some receive free lodging and food in return for their work.

VULNERABLE Weak and at risk.

ZOOLOGY The scientific study of animals.

FURTHER INFORMATION

WEBSITES

www.bats4kids.org

This website has been designed to educate children about bats. There are facts, games and other fun things to do.

www.bats.org.uk

The Bat Conservation Trust is packed with facts about bats, especially those that are found in the UK.

www.bbc.co.uk/nature/life/Pteropus

This BBC web page has information and videos about fruit bats.

www.tolgabathospital.org

Tolga Bat Hospital's official website has information about the organisation's history and the work it does.

www.youtube.com/watch?v=5FK9tWT5pA4

This video from National Geographic has footage of flying foxes in Australia.

FURTHER READING

100 Facts: Nocturnal Animals by Camilla de la Bedoyere (Miles Kelly Publishing, 2010)

Animal Neighbours: Bat by Stephen Savage (Wayland, 2007)

The Bat Scientists by Mary Kay Carson (Houghton Mifflin Harcourt, 2010)

Endangered Animals of Australia by Marie Allgor (PowerKids Press, 2011)

Eyewitness: Jungle (Dorling Kindersley, 2009)

Eyewonder: Rainforest by Helen Sharman (Dorling Kindersley, 2004)

INDEX

* Animal Rescue *

SERIES CONTENTS

BAT HOSPITAL

Tolga Bat Hospital • Trouble with Ticks • Tick Treatment • The Nursery • Hospital Workers • Health Check • Preparing Meals • Dinner Time! • The Flight Cage • Foster Care • Return to the Wild • Dangers to Bats • Reaching Out

CHIMP RESCUE

Chimp Sanctuary • Rescuing Chimps • Ngamba Island • Joining the Group • Dinner Time • The Team • Grooming • Human Friendships • Playtime! • Communication • Bedtime • Brainy Behaviour • Reaching Out

ELEPHANT ORPHANS

Elephant Nursery • Threats to Elephants • Mother's Milk • Food Supplies • Dust Baths • A New Arrival • Health Checks • Healing Touch • Elephant Friends • Off for a Walk • Playtime • Bedtime • Spreading the Word

ORANG-UTAN ORPHANS

Saving Orang-Utans • Vanishing Forests • The Pet Trade • Mums and Babies • Carers • Dinner Time • Playtime • Bedtime • Keeping Clean • Being Friendly • Forest Skills • Back to the Wild • Spreading the Word

PANDAS IN DANGER

Panda Centres • Threats to Pandas • A Diet of Bamboo • Breeding Pandas • Newborn Pandas • Feeding Time • Growing Stronger • Better Care • Ready to Explore • Keepers • Playing Outside • Panda Society • Spreading the Word

PENGUIN RESCUE

Saving Seabirds • African Penguins • Chick Rescue • On Arrival • Daily Routine • Dinner Time • From Egg to Chick • Rearing Chicks • Chick Checks • Return to the Wild • Other Birds • Black Death • Spreading the Word